I0141410

My Mind is a Mess,

This Book is Too

Written By Lynn Pittman

Acknowledgments

I have a lot of people in my life I feel I need to thank and not enough pages to do so. To friends and family who were behind me every step of the way. They helped to add to these pages with their unconditional love, their support, and their teachings.
Without these people, my book would be empty.

Table of Contents

Foreword

It is a rare privilege to see into the mind of a young person. Too often the struggle to fit in or find a place within the unsettled dynamics of the various social groups in school can erect barriers to expression. But it is an honor to see into the mind of Lynn Pittman.

Within her thoughts you will see the mask and mirror, the expression of a demanding brutality and diminishing self-critique, along with the trust and distrust of personal revelation. Through her prose you should come to appreciate and value the privilege of seeing into the mind of this gifted young person.

–   W. Fred Crow
Former columnist:
Bay Area News Group
and ANG Newspapers

Complications Of
The Heart

Throw Love into the Fire

I was drawn to him like a moth to fire
The oranges and yellows enticing me to come forth
Crackles snapping to get my attention
In the beginning of our relationship
He was the muse of my mood
Every time he laughed his sharp voice cutting through all my senses at once
The confidence radiating off of him was like the welcoming heat from a fire

I couldn't stay away
With heat comes pain
As the distance between us closed the torridity grew
The flames flaring in every direction
Engulfing me in it's intense temperature

In the end he was too possessive
and I too introspective

His name was a prayer
I worshipped every letter
If I had lit a candle every time his name came out my mouth with a smile
my room would be so luminous it would shame the sun itself

Now I spit his name out like venom
The world bursting into flame and is reduced to ash suspended in space

Flames lick the walls of my mind
Consuming my common sense
Tickling me with pain
In my brain there are images of the angry reds and oranges that accompany
a fire
The traces that there was a fire is the ash and soot left over
The black spots can be washed away after a while
But I still can't scrub away the traces of his smile

First + Last

Her body had an expiration date
long before she died.
When
          her
                    chest
                              began
                                        to
                                                  sag
and her smile lines were visible when
she wasn't smiling.

Love only lasts for so long
when it was originated from
                              lust.

When her body was young,
her hips perfectly curved have
lost their appeal.

When the end is near,
eyes close to closing
                    forever,
when she will still be smiling at rest.
She is just another person.
                                        Dead.

What is left of her is
the date of death
and
an expiration weight.

Painted Lady

There is a dog chasing me
in my dreams
I've never been able to escape his
                  jaws
Now I spend all my time washing
blood out of my thoughts

I'm bleeding so much
inside I can no longer
blush at the words you used
to tear down my walls

I've begun to stumble
ungraciously like I'm falling
for you
I knew from the start
that I was nothing more
than the rose
           between
                  my
                     legs

You have always had
your eyes on me
but it was never because
I deserved to be adored
I am nothing more
then what my body can take

I'm useless unless
I can give something
                up

When will I become a queen
instead of a pawn
I've been at the back of the board
for so long
I've begun to think I am just a referee

Heaven

My mom always said I was a gift from god
but I knew that wasn't true
How could anyone be a gift from
God
There are a million people born everyday
no one is a gift
But here I am standing
looking at you
and truly I have changed my mind

I know that God is a little lonelier now that you are here

Loose Fists

My mom always told me to stay true to me
To make sure I only attract people like me.
I think she meant that I should only
attract good people since I'm a good person.
Then why do I find myself surrounded by people I don't trust.

At first I was holding your hand,
I looked you in the eyes.
I turned to look at the beauty from around us.

I think I knew you were slipping
out of my hand but I didn't
want to hold you back.

When I turned back around
your eyes were not looking back at me.
You were gone.

I never trusted that you'd stay,
but it's whatever
I'm used to it.

I've never been one
to hold on too tightly.
Fists are always
loose.
Ready to lose

Bottled Skin

Under the surface
      So close to being seen
            Too far from being cared about

You never saw past the first layer of skin
      Never wanted to see what was underneath
            But never wanted it to be hidden from your sight.

I rub your presence from my body
      Ridding of the taint you leave behind
            Soothing myself with gentler hands

The heat dries me
      Reminding me that I shouldn't need you to make my skin glow
            Then the clouds return
                  I rely on a towel to finish what the sun promised
                  to do

Always having to return
      The water reminds me
            I'm too weak to say no to you
               Why do you have to be a perfume that
                  stains my person but disintegrates easily in
                  water

I still crave your touch
      But I don't want to deal with hating myself
            There are consequences to being in love
               Especially with a person who thinks love is between
               my thighs

Get Outta Here Wit Yo Crust Dusty A$$

You are the pesty barnacle on the bottom of my boat
Feeding off my insecurities
The only way to get you off
Is not with harsh words but
Easing you off with a skilled knife

The ache apparent
Through my day reminding me
That the love I choose
Makes me human

Up

I am a balloon
I am free in the wind
as you hold my beauty in your hands
You keep me from floating into an abyss of chaos
I don't have any boundaries
but there is an anchor that refrains me from
traveling into skies that should remain
beyond my destructive touch.

My Puzzle Pieces

Expendable Recipe

I've never belonged where I have been
I need a place that is molded to me
I need a new womb to be born from
Maybe this time the recipe will be right

2 cups of sugar instead of bitter coffee beans
Keeping me up and resentful
Instead of pounding in a pound of sarcasm
Pour in a liter of cream
To even me out and make me smooth

If the recipe I have now is the reason for my talent
It is something I'd gladly lose
Maybe with a new recipe
People will want to be around me instead of just my art

If I wasn't capable of having children I would be almost
As expendable as paper plates
Used then thrown away

But the paper plate is guaranteed to perform for you
First and only time and done with perfection
I have a life long warranty
I still may never get anything right

I Don't Make Sense

I don't make sense
I'm a dancer but naturally i'm clumsy
I talk too much but have trouble speaking up for what I believe in
I can read really fast but when it comes to that nonfiction book I have to read
for english my eyes are really tired
I can multitask but I can't text my friends and do homework at the same time
I am a Christian but curse on a regular basis
sorry God
I come up with really bad pickup lines but am surprised when they don't
work
I love everyone else but can't bear to look at myself.
I don't make sense
I can memorize every single word someone utters to me in a conversation
But I can't remember to care about your opinion
boom shade thrown
I know how to make a chocolate crepe cake
But I can't make water without burning the pot
I help everyone with their self esteem but have none of my own.
I don't make sense

Name my Conscience

My name is Yndia Geneva Lynn Pittman yet that is not who I am.
I may go by those names but those names
do not hold me.
They are other people
people I have never wanted to be.
People I could never find myself looking up to.
Like the little girl named Yndia that helped my brother as a baby.
She is who my mom expected me to be.
The expectation to be a good person crafted before I was even born.
She was Yndia.
My mom just hoped to transfer her kindness to me

Why have a name if you will just call me something else.
I am not India with an I or Yindia.
Every time a teacher sees my name for the first time their face
scrunches up in thought.
"Should I just guess or just look for someone who looks as if this
would be their name?"
Their eyes fall on me.
"Y-Yindia?"
"Yea sure."
I have become accustomed to being someone other than myself
Either laughed at and ridiculed for the name given to me
Or treated as a special student because "I don't know how to spell my
name"

In 7th grade my history teacher said later in the period that I had to go
to the office to change my name on Powerschool because It was
obviously wrong.

I was a freshman and I ran track. The coach never called me by my name he just said "Hey Frederick's little sister"
I would roll my eyes and get ready.
The only time he got even remotely close to my name
was when I got 1st place in 200 meters and he started calling me "Yndi500".
I quit later that week.

My mom's reason for giving me these names is because she wanted to pay tribute to beautiful women.
My mom's reasoning for giving me these names is not good enough.
She should've changed her own goddamn name.
A name isn't for the benefit of your guilty conscience.
It should be me.

I am tired of being called exotic, Indian, India like the country.
I am tired of being called something that has never belonged to me truly.
I am not a little girl consoling a baby
I am not one of the grandmothers I've never met
I am someone unique

I deserve something better than a hand-me-down.

Paper Cut Out

I look in the
mirror
my ribs make me look
symmetrical
my meaning of life is
torn to shreds
within me

I kill myself on the inside
It doesn't show on the outside

baggy sweaters
became a trend
at 6
I stand in front of
my reflection
praying to be
someone better

She told me I was fat
Fat is not beautiful

I question
who I am with
fingers tearing
my throat

the acid burns
my brain into pieces
of anger and queasiness
my wrists fit neatly
in my own hands

The smile on my face is
diminished to a memory

my mind paints the masterpiece
of who I will be if I
just feel a little more pain
fatigue sits next to me
in class

I have died within the paradox
of my mind
The commitment of life in the future
is now only a moral choice

Color Me A Rainbow

My wrists used to be stained red
Not with my blood But with the ink
I used to paint the canvas
my skin
then ran out of ink and never drew again

I've been drowning in orange
I fucking hate orange
yet here I am
living in a town
where the school colors
are orange

I have always been called little yellow girl
Not because I bring sunshine where I step
but because my color of skin
needed to be degraded
By my own family
they mean it lovingly but still

My town is the epitome of green
Each tree or bush a different shade
but all meaning one thing
That this place was full of life
and healthy
Well, that was how it looks on the surface
Tear back the bark and you
can see it is rotted to the core
Only able to stand straight because
we will it to
Not so perfect under the cover of porcelain skin

The sky has learned to change
itself depending on how it feels

Sounds kind of like me
You would think that it would only
change several shades of blue
instead I've seen the sky
adopt a new skin
and put it on like it was always there

My favorite color is purple
I love how it is the hardest color to see
on the spectrum
my favorite color can also kill me
just by shining on my form
gotta love those ultra violet rays

I'm Alive Here

The walls inside are cracked
and are just holding on
They remind me of you

No matter how much glue or love I use
both walls and you are in danger
of being destroyed by your own experiences

In every room my voice and footsteps echo
I feel uncomfortable with my own existence
so I stop walking and talking
I listen to the natural sounds of an old building
complaining under the weight of its many years of use

I have spent the weekend
breathing in the ocean air
and exhaling peace

I swim in the ocean confidently
My fear of being eaten by a shark
is eased when I am able to relinquish control of my body

I imagine being intertwined with a personified love
Us dancing
kicking up sand
becoming one

I wrote
"I was alive here"
in the sand

People think it's funny
but it is a final statement
I hope that someone sees it
and knows that
in my whole life
I finally felt alive

I am Different

My alter ego made me realize that I am a very sad person
I struggled to put a smile on my face and talk in a southern accent and
deliver with precision
with the happiness I said I had
It took too much energy to pretend to be happy
I just kept wishing to stop
stop smiling
stop talking
I wanted the pretending to stop

When I went back to being "myself"
I found I was still pretending
I hate my laugh
I just want to stop laughing
but every night
I tell myself it is better to sacrifice my comfort for
everyone's happiness

No one likes a depressed person
no one wants their issues

I wish to sit in the house
and watch red rain pitter patter on a window
Maybe the rain isn't red
maybe I'm using the wrong glass pane
or the wrong eyes

I always feel I am living in the wrong body
Each step clumsy and almost sending me to my knees
I feel like an alien
Maybe it's because I wish I wasn't human

I stood in Goodwill and a man asked me
if anyone had ever tried kidnapping me

because I'm so beautiful

"You so
            gorgeous girl.
                        You wearing
                                    high heels
                                                are you a big girl now?"

"No, sir. I'm 14."

That was a couple months ago
I'm actually 18 but I hope by saying I'm younger
they will realize what they are saying is wrong
they will realize that they do not own me
they will realize they don't win me
just by calling me beautiful
You have to work a little harder than that

I was supposed to have lunch with friends but after 15 minutes I convinced
myself I wasn't a friend of theirs.
 I gave her money and had panic attack walking through Oakland.

My last words will either be
"eat cheese and potato quesadillas at my funeral"
Or
"love someone else today"
because they always love you more in your last moments

This school was the best and worst thing that
happened in my life
I learned the only way to fit in here
is to pretend

I have to stop pretending that I love my words
I don't

Rhythmic Blindness

I have always treated my glasses as though they only cost a couple of bucks but in all actuality, they are precious and were dearly missed when they broke and I was forced to endure everything without full sight. Every shape is taking up more space than it should. If I had glasses I could see the defined crisp lines that are their edges.

In my house everything has grown and has become a monster waiting for me to take my inadequate eyes off of it. I have lived in my town for 16 years but it astounds me that as soon as my glasses are off, everything is ominously new and unfamiliar. On the train every shadow is a threat. Sight is taken for granted by a lot of people including me. I get anxious when walking around people without my glasses because even though I know that they have facial features like eyes and mouths, I am seeing faceless strangers with their attention on me even if they don't have their head turned.

Usually when I walk down the street I smile at those who pass me, but without my glasses they are more of a stranger to me than if I could see their eyes crinkle with a smile or the face turn up at my existence. The unknown expressions makes me doubt myself.

Every word I type is wrong even if it happens to be right. My eyes constantly trying to focus on something as I am running through my day. The fatigue starting in my eyes and leaking into my brain and down my spine branching out.

The Holes Inside

Abyss in the Eyes

I am a failure
in the eyes of the people
who created me

I am alone
in a school where
your popularity depends
on your social life

I am useless
unless someone
wants something

I am disappearing
into an abyss
of depression
and no one
notices anything

One day they will look up
and I won't be here
Everyone abandoned
me
when I needed them
most
One day I'll be gone
nothing left but my
ghost

Blind Daggers

I hold the head of happiness to my face
The saying is
"Cut off one head and two more appear in its place"
I thought happiness would give birth to hope and confidence
or something like that

I didn't expect depression and loneliness
to grow from the shoulders of life

Life is kneeled before me
as I chop head after head
searching for positivity in this cruel being

Only my eyes peek out from beneath
all the self destroying decisions I've made

I've been looking for a prism of light
shining in the darkest corners of everything
looking for a rainbow to go to the other side of
and find a bucket of hope

Even paintings can't capture
the art of losing all
that made you human

Teeth of ice bite into my naivety
and swallow the innocence
leaving behind a bitter, empty shell

Clouds of a storm that has
been brewing for years and is now
overflowing from my head
Shriveled to nothing but a coal of cold regret

I learned to fight bullies when I was younger
but the war I never win
is the one in my mind
Littering my mind with bodies
of self esteem and confidence

I'm shot down when trying
to escape my brain
Dreams slowly bleeding out

Now I kneel before life
A dagger in his hand at my throat
Whispering for me to end my own life
with my own desperation for a light
at the end of this endless tunnel
It was a headlight
I never saw the truth coming at me
As I hurled myself headfirst
into the abyss
that life sends you

Lonely

1
2
3
4
5
Feet between people
I have made a hobby of counting how much space
is between me and everyone else
My mind knows it is just a way for me to fall
into the never ending cycle again
but I can't help it
This hobby of mine makes me think
of all the reasons why I am
The last person people want to love

Cringe worthy jokes
Annoying
My intelligence to them is just reasonable stupidity
I talk too much
I am too good at multitasking
And yes I was told this
I didn't know you could be too good at multitasking
but I guess I am

My humor is too dark for others to grasp hold of
They don't understand when
I have to laugh at my own jokes to fill the silence
I am laughing at my
existence
because maybe if I didn't exist everyone would
smile and laugh a little more
maybe I am blocking the happiness of others

I've tried being that girl
That girl everyone gets along with
That person who's smile looks so easy and natural
That person you would love to say hi to in the hallway

I never got close
My smile has never looked easy
I'm too much of a bitter person to be able
to let my lip slide across
my face in an arc of genuine happiness

Why am I in the margins
of my own story
I wish that I could be the main character
but knowing me
I have already cast someone else in that role

I sit far from people
to be able to feel part of anything
I still try to be someone others want to be around
I give people more than what they ask for
I hug endlessly even if I really don't like touching
I listen to people cry and make them laugh through my tears

I do all these things but they are never remembered
or cherished like I want to be
So I have yet to try and sit closer
than
1
2
3
4
5
Feet from all the people that
I love

Perched Above Despair

The bark was cutting
into the palm of my hand.
the pain was welcoming

The verbal missiles launched
At my perch.
there was no escape
The tears in my eyes created a
waterfall

Static Thoughts

I have cupped my mind in my hands
Gazing at the pieces that have darkened with the anguish
I have learned to spot the rare pastel colors
I place my brain back in
Hearing static and screams

Aim Higher

Desert Love

as long as there was a child
we were eternally here.
my genes are not pure:
torn from
women without consent,
bloomed from the cracks everyone
avoided.

Is this making you unstable.

I am nothing but the dust
you kick up when you dance.
me swirling alongside you.

The land didn't want me anymore
sands giving birth
to scorpions who come for the weak

Bleeding Dreams

My life was supposed to matter from the beginning,
instead at 17 I have to scream that truth at the top of my lungs.
I have to validate my own existence
because you couldn't find the space in your closed mind to
realize that my life actually matters.

My race is filled with bullets
and we are watering the earth with the
lost dreams you have torn from our
broken bodies.

For generations you have been violently
taking us away from our families.

We don't want to be better than anyone,
we just want to be alive like everyone else
and stay that way.

A Milk Carton Dreams

Help
I'm missing
Have you seen me

No you have not because you don't look for colored skin that even resembles
the rich earth that supports you

Help
I've been hurt
Did you report my absence

No you haven't because if I was hurt it must have been my fault

Help
I feel invisible
Did you look for me

No you haven't because you know where I am
You are the one who trapped me here
With the cops and judges pointing their finger saying guilty

I'm not supposed to be here
I've grown too large and intelligent to be in this
6 by 8 ft coffin you call a prison cell

Someone else's demons have caught up with me
2 years later
And I am spending my time here

When someone says your name
It feels intimate
Validating your existence
And telling you that you are real

Do you know my name
Or is it just a picture of me
I'm missing and only a milk carton knows

The truth shall set you free

They took you once
They came back to finish you.
The truth is only revealed when our bones
are dust beneath your feet
your struggle to wade through our pain.
my silent screams haunt

Frozen Liveliness

Inside our body is a light
captures all darkness and freezes it
No matter the body in which our light is contained
it shines through.

We oppress what we love
so that we may prove to others
we are no different
that there is something to hate about us too.
We squander our own happiness in hopes it will make us happy.
The common sense evades us.

Love is something we all have
yet don't trust enough to give.
Hate has been sewed into our genetics
preventing us from openly sharing our souls with the world.

Me v Society

<u>Dear _____</u>,

      If you are female do not feel proud about the added flesh given to you by God. You have one job and that is to give the world children. You may be beautiful but remember that beauty is an accessory. You are here to bring balance to the world with your feelings, but you are not here to run it. Because, if the world was run by people who have sympathy and love and compassion the world would be a better place and I can't make money from love. Maybe I could but it is easier to let the world be run by men that make the rest of society grovel for the approval that they provide.

      If you are an African American do not have children. If your skin is darker than a tan do not feel proud. Do not remember that your ancestors were kings and queens because you are not in the eyes of society. You stick out like a sore thumb. No you stick out like you don't belong. I can't find love in you because I have been taught that you are lower than me. Everyone has a role to play. Your job is to disappear because we made a mistake when we brought you here to serve us and you gained enough knowledge to serve yourself. This society was not created to help the black community; it was created to encourage white supremacy. This nation is not for you. The United states of a Divided People.

Sincerely,

Society

Dear Society,

This is the year I become a legal adult, but some things that come with being an adult, mind you, a black female adult, will not be a surprise to me. Because I have already been belittled because of my sex. I have been told that I was born to bring forth a child. I refuse to be used like a cow, the only reason I am alive is because I must give a man what he wants. I don't need to have a baby to meet some quota just to make someone else feel as though they have created something. I was raised by a woman who was born and then treated like a burden. I will never bring a life into this world if I cannot guarantee that her life will be one where she is loved. Today is a new day and gender is only a suggestion but why is even the suggestion of my gender a negative one?

I am black and I am sick and tired of being told that my life matters when that statement is being countered with gunfire and the killer being let off. You shouldn't have to publicly validate my existence just so you can look as if you were on my side the whole time. I refuse to be mindful of the boundaries you made for us. I will break free of my mental bonds and provide you with the truth you tried to squander with your hate and your cleverly crafted stereotypes fabricated to unravel me. I will assemble myself and give my tools to all to manufacture what we were destined to be since the beginning. Free.

-Lynn Pittman

Empathic Sounds of Living in a War

The ocean of wind around us makes us become a community.
One blanket to shelter us from the war and the hate it brings.
The crackling of our bones matches the sound of the fire.

The fire that burns in each of us
the fire that we will pass on

you started the war
but we will rise and be
victorious

Cold

"What did life teach you yesterday?"

If you stay outside too long body parts will turn blue.
Body no longer shivering because the cold has already saturated my blood.
My fingertips try to type "play
That is my dying wish.

I learned that the cold can be as painful as heat.
Everyone forgets what freezing temperatures can do to a person.
Sure heat can make someone unrecognizable,
But the cold kills and then preserves so all can see the pain the person felt as
they died.

Los Gatos

Los Gatos you are beautiful
You are covered in trees that cool me
Sweat waterfalls over your body creating
streams to be dipped into
The curves of your streets are
washed once a week to keep you clean

Los Gatos you are a bitch
Every clean street I stand on makes
me feel unwelcome
I stop traffic
and I sure as hell know it is
not because I'm pretty

If you peel the bark off of
one of your many trees
the confederate flag is carved into the layers
telling me how long racism has been lying under
your flawless skin
It tells me that when this tree grows more
it will keep covering it up
but it will always be there.

My skin has become
the indicator of if I succeed

You're culture will only be mocked
behind your back

Immersed in Red

I've been convicted of a crime
The crime of being an artist
I have looked at the world in a difference lense
That lense being a more colorful lense

I am immersed in a red jumpsuit
and I have escaped a hell
My hell was a place I was oppressed
for loving a world where life included
creativity
and achieving happiness was feasible

I have been handed a rainbow ball filled with razors
and it fills me with conflict
How am I supposed to hand this burden of
lies and fake smiles to someone else
like it was done to me

To Live and Die in Oakland

I wasn't born here but my life has been changed here
I spent most of my childhood
feeling like I was below the surface of the earth
I was never seen
therefore I couldn't breathe

There is so much life in Oakland
it's filled with so much color
including mine
Making me relevant in the plethora of shades

I was finally able to fill my lungs with air
with peace
When I cry here it actually means something
It's not overlooked
Every tear is caught
the dreams extracted and given back to me

I used to be afraid of dying
when spending time in Los Gatos
My brown body would rot
in the dirt I look like

Now dying doesn't seem that bad
My light will go out in a city
blanketed in the warmth of a chaotic unity

At first I thought that I would feel pain in Oakland
Instead my skin is glowing
In Oakland I am beautiful
In Los Gatos I am a burden

To live and die in Oakland is to
Live and be loved forever

Drum Walk

The african drums were supposed to be the heartbeat of the black body.
The body was supposed to sway to that beat,
moving along the streets kicking up dust with our natural rhythm
but instead we had to manufacture our own rhymes.
Make hip hop and swag walks that we feel leaning our body to the side.

We had to build ourselves from the dirt you said we were lower than
We created a united love from the divided people you supplied us with.

tHe **AIR** inside my head

Hell isn't under my feet. It is something I take with me wherever I go. I am tangled in it's net, woven by the strands sprouting from my mind. We are poisoned at a young age to hate the way we look. You can always be thinner, bustier, smarter, stronger. But no one has turned out perfect, even with all the pills and potions shoved down our throats through advertisements.

Everyone's hell is fabricated in different places. It may be the salon chair. The longer you sit the more recognition you get.

Hail the things that bring us down
Around us are cues we aren't good enough
It is the thing we obsess about
Round and round we go inside our minds

My hell was created between the thighs of the women who said they love me. Fingers pulling at my nerves and my self-esteem. Pain is beauty. That line fuels many people to torture themselves. Trying to look like the models in magazines. We will never look like them because we are not the same. We were born different and we should remain that way. In nature it is very rare to see the same thing twice.

Go Further

Find My Dreams Squashed By Your Motives

My dad told me he was going to move to Africa. Specifically Ghana because someone said they were giving land to former slaves and helping them come home. My dad said there is so much white evil here and it's burning every shred of humanity we thought we had, and making it a distant memory. He thinks my brother and I are too tainted to be saved. So he is jumping ship and abandoning us to die in the collapsing world white people have created. I don't exactly blame him for his decision. I'm pissed that he would rather adopt new kids and raise them "the right way" instead of loving us here. But that's beside the point. The idea that I am filled with white evil makes sense in a way, if only to me. I'm light skinned and I have been called satan's spawn many times. My dad decided that he would jump out of the society here and jump into Africa's and pursue the American dream there. He still longs for the perfect wife and kids with a white picket fence but he thinks he can't pursue that here without challenges. What is really difficult to understand is there will be challenges there but I guess he has the right idea since race won't be such a big factor in his success rate. At least on the surface that doesn't seem like it will be a problem. Hopefully in Ghana the black people don't have black on black crime. Maybe it is just an American thing.

I don't think there can be a new American dream because if people are trying to find ways to escape the collapse of the U.S. like my dad then we are too far gone. To implement a new American dream is to erase the old one from not only current Americans but also other countries, because that is one of the reasons they come here. In our U.S. History classes we learn how other countries thought of the U.S. and why they would decide to come here. Like immigrants used to hear that the U.S. had streets paved with gold. The U.S. was seriously put on a pedestal. Of course we don't have the same status as we used to but immigrants still come here hoping to acquire success they couldn't get back where they originally come from. Not for totally awesome individualistic ideals and a below-average implied societal hierarchy. They, like us, want happiness except they will travel to a foreign land and suffer through the everyday American hate and judgement to get a taste of it and give it to the ones they love.

It's hard to imagine a new American dream not because there is nothing better than our country, but because the formed society has deteriorated so much that we have buried ourselves under so much hatred and poisonous misconstrued values, we can't dig ourselves. It would take a big a miracle to make my dad change his mind and actually try to be my father instead of the sperm donor and an even bigger miracle to create and put into place a new American dream.

We can't force people to stay in our lives so we don't suffer from the knowledge that they are absent. We can't force people to actually have the understanding that we need to be communal instead of looking at everyone as individuals. We shouldn't have to create a law or new dream of equal success based on how we work together. It should be common sense that working together makes us stronger. But I guess common sense isn't really common.

U.S. in 200 years

I wake up and snort. The orange air smells toxic but that's normal. I roll out of bed and stumble my enlarged chest dragging me down slightly. When I regain my balance I wipe the sleep from my eyes I wade through my apartment. Take a deep breath of air before starting my way downstairs which was completely immersed in water. My lungs are very large so I can stay underwater for around 10 minutes. It takes 5 minutes to get my breakfast. My toes spread apart like wings and the webbing between my toes helps me quickly swim to the kitchen. I go to the clear refrigerator and pick out what i want. I pick out a breakfast bar and applesauce. I type what I want into the refrigerator door and immediately the food is transferred into a water tight food holder. The slider turns around and lets me grab the food. When the food is safely into my hand the slider turns back around and I watch as the cubby drains the water that was let in when I grabbed my food. I have had this refrigerator for two years and it still amazes me how it drains the water. I look into my refrigerator's water bag to see if it needs to be emptied. It does.

I flip up the switch on my fridge so that someone comes to pick it up. I then swim back upstairs and breathe in the orange air. I change my pajama wetsuit and put on a casual workplace wetsuit. I walk out the front door with my hand wrapped tightly around the packaged food. I step into the fire proof boots set outside my door. I lace them up tightly. My cousin Carl had forgotten to lace them tightly and when he walked over the lava highway some lava seeped into his shoes. The webbing between the toes are now the achilles heels of humans. He died two minutes before the WWWP, World Wide Web Patrol, could pick him up. His body solidified into ice then he melted into water in record time. Most of the time it takes two hours but I guess the heat made him melt in 10 minutes. Now there is a permanent dark spot where he died and he cooled the lava into a hard rock. Every time I pass his spot I thank him for the tiny piece of land he provided with his life.

Finding Futures in a Tragic Present

I wonder
What life would be like
In the future

Would people care more about
their bank accounts
More than about other people's well-being still
or will they have learned that the only way
to succeed as a species
is to have the common sense to control
their urges to be more successful than their neighbor

Will people still kill each other based on
their religion or race
because they were born with parents
who feel threatened by other people who
have done nothing to deserve the hate
or will everyone finally figure out that
in the grand scheme of things race and religion
don't matter because we eventually all die
and the things we leave behind
are the only things we pass on to be remembered by

Or maybe none of that happens because the world deteriorates
so much that it goes into survival
the primal idea of every man for himself put into effect
the world doing away of any traces of humans
trying to scrub itself clean of all the poisons
we decided to inject into its beautiful surface

Crucified Belonging

Buried in Sin

This coffin is getting smaller
All the lies I've told choking me
False words clotting my throat

Nails pounded deep in the wood
holding my prison together under all the dirt I've done

I want to scream
but my lips burn
The same lips I used to torture boy after boy
Promising kisses but giving none

My brain is burning with images I should feel guilty about
Fingertips grazing sacred flesh
Nails digging wounds into skin that doesn't belong to me

My knuckles are bleeding from all
the people I have raised my fist against

My wrist pours blood into a goblet
My cup runneth over

Slowly but surely
every demon I have awoken is catching up with me
dragging me deeper into the depths of my hell

Still Waiting for my Wings

I have been praying
for guidance
for so long
Too long

My life has passed by me
waiting for a sign that God
cares and loves me

I did my best to meet Him
halfway
but I always found myself
tripping on my
inability to trust
in Him and in myself
falling short of what He wants
Kind of makes sense
I am pretty short

I feel like
I am on a treadmill
trying to keep up with the
continuously increasing speed
of what is ok in the
condescending eyes of Him
Trying to find the stop button so I can take a breath

How can He love me when He created
me so flawed
It says in the bible that we were created in His image
        Does He get His period every month?
                Does He suffer from depression and self hate?
        Is He really as fucked up as we are?

Obviously He is
because he was the cause of the first couple of genocides
We just picked up where He left off
we started killing each other in His name.
And then out of His name
It was a cycle of hate and murder that he started

Maybe I am like the devil having
Gone against the word of God and
Being cast aside like the scum that falls from heaven

If God loved us so much
He would have just kept us in his heavenly palace
We are all fallen angels He would rather throw away
And keep the best to himself

I hit the ground
covered in the corruption of the world
the world was already ready to taint the wings of my innocence

But honestly I was already as tainted as the rest were

Splintered Embers

I am a fire
Slowly dying out
Water trickling down
Onto my life
In the shape of religion

I look at the bible
And think
I'll never be good enough
To make it to His kingdom

It says that
You have to confess
And give yourself to
Him genuinely and completely

I've never been able to do that
I have so many doubts about God
And His motives.
He has never been there
For me so why should
I feel the need to give
My life to God

My church leaders tell me
Sometimes you
Have to give your life
In order to clearly see His
Miracles happening in your life

The only miracle I see in my
Life is the fact that I am not dead yet
But that is more human error
Never getting the amount of pills right

Then finally just not having enough
Energy to go through with killing myself

My faith has always been
On a shaky foundation
The ground shifting
Throwing me to my knees
Time and time again
Looking for deliverance

I Don't Even Know

Junkless

The Bart train came to a hard stop. I noticed that people clutched things in fear. And I knew that the thing they clung to, oh so tightly, was in that moment the most important thing to them.

Most of the people around me grabbed at a pole or a hoop to keep themselves from falling. They were grabbing their pride so they didn't drop it.

I witnessed a man grab his junk. I think he was either trying to keep his manhood from plummeting to the piss covered floor or was extremely excited and didn't want anyone to know.

I saw a mother hold her child close. Sacrificing her comfort so they wouldn't feel pain.

And me. I didn't grab anything. I let myself plunge and hit the ground so it could grab onto me.

Your Fan

I pleasure you when you turn me on. When you say I love you I only hum back in response. When you push my buttons because I stop abruptly I say nothing to stop you. When you hug me tight on those hot summer nights I do nothing but work hard for you. Through the years when everyone leaves you, I am the only one that stays put. Somedays you just push me aside like I am a heavy burden and other days you gingerly place me in front of you like I am the only thing in the universe that matters. Sometimes I spin, canvassing the room for you but you have left once again. Other times I am stable, facing you and watching as you work. I am nothing to you but everything at the same time. I don't really mind. After all I'm just your biggest fan.

Jump Dust

I know that I will not be one of the stars that float effortlessly in space.

I will not travel past the sun and be adorned by its light

I know that my feet will remain on solid ground

I know that the farthest I will going to the sky is how high I can jump

I jump and for a split second I'm flying

then I am back on the ground

my feet covered in earth and dust

I stand looking up at the great beyond

with my feet smashing clay

Abstract

You can tell when you look at the paper that it's a mess
Everything not really having meaning and blending into other things on the canvas abruptly
The canvass reflects my mind.
There is a mess of numbers, images, words, and aimless lines.
There is no direction
No order
My mind reflects my life
I live on the streets
I have no direction
There is nothing stable about my life except the concrete ground I sleep on
All I see are people walking around me in all directions
Speaking aimless words that mean nothing to me but everything to them
They are a mess of fast and slow moving bodies.
I see a sorts of signs as I wander about.
I've seen so many that they all mix together
A mess of letters and numbers
There are straight lines
Just jagged cracks in the sidewalks I sleep on and misplaced puzzle pieces of bark that are attached to the tree I seek to find shelter from the rain.
I capture all of the things around me and I place them on a canvass

Tainted by Human Lives

There seems to be more treachery passing through me
Than what was already there when I was created
Through the years I have learned to just let the bullshit pass on my screen
I feel tainted by what flashes over me day by day.
One day it is peaceful and someone is saving a dog
The next day two boys have died
because they didn't meet someone's standard of humanity
I'm glad I'm not human and I am just a television

Twinkle Tums

The tips of my fingers reach for objects that don't exist
I sway as if to music
Letting my body be pushed and pulled
by spiritual forces

My stomach glides from my body
and takes the stage for a solo dance
It leaps across the stage
I leap towards the bathroom

There is a ringing in my ears
The shrill melody the organs boogie to
My heart in my esophagus creating
an unwelcome and uncoordinated beat

As I lie down and roll around the bed
trying to quiet my soul the
"Slide to the left, Slide to the right,"
rages inside
As soon as it gets to the criss-cross
I am on the floor gasping
Maybe air will neutralize the threat

Anchored to Reality

What is Left?

My family is split
Fear runs through half but disbelief runs through all
We are no longer connected through views
But only connected by blood

All my dad has left is a car that moans as he drives
His backseat is a bed
Full of tools and anxiety

All my mom has left is the monthly trips
When she gets home she plans for another one
Packing her suitcase full of vodka and regret

All my brother has left is video games and work
Spending as much time at home
trying to fill his time
With excuses and distractions

All I have left is my voice
I use it to pretend
that I am alive

Promises

My mom never makes a promise
at least not a promise she can't keep
maybe that is why she has never
promised me
that she will be there when I want her to be there

She promised to take my phone for the rest of the year
if I got a bad grade
she kept her promise
and I haven't seen it since

My dad makes a lot of promises
he has promised to be there for a lot of my events
he has yet to keep his promise
something always comes up
he will always take a job
over coming to see me do something
he probably will never see me do again

My brother learned his lesson
and never makes a promise he can't keep
he avoids making promises as much as possible
I'm never too sure with him
He will either show up or he won't
but you won't know until it is too late

Suffering at it's Finest:
a.k.a School

White Bombardment

I have found that I am surrounded by white
When I left Los Gatos I thought
I had escaped
The white buildings
With their white walls
Filled with white people
Surrounding me in a constant bombardment
Of people who aren't me

I came here to
Feel as if I belonged
That lasted for a year
Then the truth set in

The white walls here are scarred and yellowed
 with hand prints
Artistic hands trying
to create a way out of this suffocating
Box of expectations and regulations
Trying to escape from conforming
to society's standards

This school may be filled with people
who don't follow society's rules
But society still rules the school
We've lost teachers who should be kept

We are slowly fading into
The darkness which is normality
We are holding on by our fingertips
Still trying to grasp at our creativity

But slowly our colorful murals
Are disappearing and are just becoming
White walls
To white buildings
That hold us against our will

Emma's Voice

I couldn't hear her voice but i could see it
I could see the sorrow and anger billowing from her lips
As her chest heaved with each breath it took to try to save future lives
She held the eyes of all as she gave her testimony
She held the eyes of the world as she filled the air with a heavy silence
6 minutes was all it took for lives to be taken
How many more minutes, hours, years
Will it take before her voice and the silence she brought is not just
something that haunts us
But has pushed the world to make a change.

The atmosphere was pregnant with silence as she cried
For all the students who will never get the joy and the fear from pregnancy

Their bodies are not filled with new lives
They are filled bullets

Her voice is filled with anger
And hope
That one day living will not be a questionable thing to students

Sounds of OSA

I sit in the halls and listen to the simultaneous sounds of normalcy and talent
The girls talk about nonsense and then take a moment to harmonize
The boys' deep voices ring through the air with glee and in the background
you can hear a guitar being strummed
The lazy talent is burned into the walls
Even I am playing solitaire as I write this
The sounds are overwhelming and calming at the same time
The flow of OSA is staccato and legato all at the same time
Able to make music of its own chaos

Sounds of LGHS

Ah Los Gatos High School
the only sounds I heard were
of racist bullshit,
and the bell ringing
the day was never over fast enough

Rick Santorum

How dare you
My generation is filled with bullets and you think CPR will fix it
My generation is watering the earth with blood
And you think CPR will fix it

You think CPR will save my life
when the lead boils in my stomach
I am saving my life by protesting the laws
you created to protect your land
Your land is no longer under attack
so why do you still need them
Your children are under attack
yet
you think that your guns
have more worth than their lives

Differences Can Make us Weak

In different places we are taught different things
In los Gatos High the students are taught to step on anyone
and everyone's shoulders to get to the top
In San Jose Elementary they are taught to pick
something easy and not to have too many expectations
In OSA we are taught to achieve each and
every goal that comes to our minds and not settle for anything less
In Ohio they taught my dad to just
get as far away from the bipolar weather as soon as possible
In East Palo Alto they taught my mom
that the only way to get anything in life is to take it.
I taught myself that all of those qualities are good sometimes
Sometimes you need to use the resources that others supply you with

Remember Me

Young Perspective of Things

FRONT PORCH

I am 8 as I sit on the front porch. My toes are cold as I look across the street as the girls jumped on a trampoline. Their almost artificial squeals filled the air. I slowly cut my eyes from them by wiggling my toes, trying to get the appendages to snap like their cousins, the fingers. I was used to being alone and trying to entertain myself. My mom was burdened with work and school. I knew at that age my happiness would have to wait. I would sit on the front step looking at the scenery that I loved even though I had seen it every day since we got there in 2002, 6 years earlier. Home was a place of quiet. My brother and I despised each other and avoided communicating in anyway. I was the annoying little sister that was needy and always wanted to play and be loved. I'm sure it was extremely aggravating.

BEDROOM

I spent most of my free time in my bed. It has always been my punishment. When my mom couldn't deal with my emotional 12 year old state she would tell me to go to bed and sleep off my bad mood. I learned that in order to stay part of the family emotions are to stay off you face and off your heart and in the back of your mind until only your head is filled with the emotions you could never express. That is until the dam breaks and the flood of emotions forces your loved ones to confront your issues. I still hold back my emotions and have exploded twice. I am definitely sure the next time I explode will be soon because I already feel the tell tale sign. My right eye starts to twitch and every time I feel stressed in anyway air flees from my body and a nerve in my head is pulled taut. I was fragile as I lay in bed letting tears run down my face onto the pillow there was almost no time that it was good to talk to my mom about my problems. All I could do is look in the mirror and watch myself disintegrate and wonder if my family saw my decline in life.

LIVING ROOM

My mom thought it would be a great idea to have thursday night movie nights. So we all climbed onto her bed aka the couch and sat pretended we enjoyed each other's company while watching a movie that was way too funny for our comically serious family. We loved each other but we didn't like each other. We knew who the other person was so we didn't feel the need to be close. I always attempted to sit in a chair next to the couch but always ended being pressured into sitting in middle of my mom and brother. I have never liked touching my family so sitting in such close proximity to them made me extremely uncomfortable and I prayed for the torture to stop. I wasted no time in saying I was tired and escaping to the darkness of the room I shared with my brother. Solitary is where I found peace and depression. What a shitty mix.

Proud

In 1st grade I went to school in San Jose. It was called Stipe Elementary. At lunch I usually ate alone which was kinda the norm. One day I was eating alone and a girl and her friends came to sit next to me. I was and am a very paranoid kid so I didn't trust them from the start. One of the girls took my white milk and switched it with her chocolate milk and said, " You are black so you should drink chocolate milk." I was no stranger to racist comments at that school so I grabbed the chocolate milk held it over her almost white hair and with all my strength crushed the carton and all the milk spilled over her hair. She gasped and squealed as the milk gushed over her silky hair making it look dirty and ugly. I then grabbed her hair by the roots and proceeded drag her around the, very large, cafeteria by her hair with her screaming. I didn't let go until the bell rang and when I let go a considerable amount of hair was still almost glued to my palm by the sticky milk and the sweat that had 15 minutes to develop.

Your Own

If my book has inspired you, allow me to be your muse and use this space to write your own thoughts or poem.

_____

_____

_____

_____

_____

_____

_____

_____

_____

_____

_____

_____

_____

_____

_____

_____

_____

_____

_____

_____

To learn more about this author visit

pittmanportfolio.com

Contact Info:
(408) 475-8983
yndiaglp@gmail.com

www.ingramcontent.com/pod-product-compliance
Lightning Source LLC
Chambersburg PA
CBHW031326040426
42443CB00005B/228